Tugging on My Heart Strings

Sheila Nielsen

BookLeaf Publishing

Tugging on My Heart Strings © 2023 Sheila Nielsen

All rights reserved.

No part of this publication may be reproduced, stored in a retrieval system, or transmitted, in any form or by any means, electronic, mechanical, photocopying, recording or otherwise, without the prior written permission of the presenters.

Sheila Nielsen asserts the moral right to be identified as author of this work.

Presentation by *BookLeaf Publishing*

Web: www.bookleafpub.com

E-mail: info@bookleafpub.com

ISBN: 9789357445863

First edition 2023

The Spirit of the Staircase

A staircase is a haunting place
with fears and dreams on either end
uncertain if the darkness behind
will catch me before I reach the light

I'm not ready for who or what awaits
Perhaps in my uncertainty, I am the darkness
Youth was so easy with bright flames of hope
and I always held the lantern and lit the way

But obscurity looms with greater intensity
Lights in my life are smudged out one by one
Pinpoints of confidence and security gone
now lost in a void of intense darkness

Spirit of the Staircase, speak gently to me
Were youthful wanderings blissfully obscured
with symbolism and meaning lost to my eyes
ignorant to how short my staircase may be

I have spent two-thirds of my life in the staircase
uncertain how to manage my last third with
grace
give me strength and courage to find joy in
ambiguity

Assure me, Spirit ~ the light ahead waits to welcome me

After the Winter

Spring emerges in all her splendor
    Awakening souls from winter's repose
Teasing and tickling our sensory wonder
    Happily blooming beneath our toes
Winter is now a fleeting memory
    Today the sun, a welcomed delight
Whilst breezes sweep us up in reverie
    All stress and care adrift in flight

And let us stroll along the lane
    With trees in bud and bloom
As birds delight in sweet refrain
    Adorned for mates in gorgeous plume
Arise, my love, and join my song
    Be mine as seasons come and go
We'll walk together forever strong
    Again, renewed in spring's fresh glow

Writing is Power

As a writing teacher
I challenge my students
to lift their voices
and discover that writing is power

It takes courage
meeting new students
and introducing objectives
as a writing teacher

But that is my role
my chosen avocation
to be a mentor and
I challenge my students

I set personal goals
instead of driven agendas
inspiring young scholars
to lift their voices

It is an amazing breakthrough
Putting thoughts on paper
to build confidence with words
and discover that writing is power

Angels Surround Us

There is something quite lovely
about living in a small town
a place where I am recognized
on the sidewalk, in a shop or at a store.

Familiar names and faces of friends
sharing smiles and greetings
both sweet and genuine
often offered with a tender hug

I wonder if this is a glimpse of heaven
in which the connections of heart and soul
far outweigh the ugliness of humanity
that lurks in dark and scary corners.

Shouldn't our actions always be
in the way we choose to love others?
Can't we dispose of biases and bigotry
in favor of happiness, joy and love?

Perhaps heaven isn't a place
It might be that heaven is a feeling
Slow down, my friend, and see
the angels who surround us

Disconnected

I sit on the bench
watching people walk by
Most are looking down
at their phones,
plugged in to connect
while being completely
disconnected from the world
around them

They miss the beautiful chirrup of birds
the rumble of approaching wheels on the scooter
the chimes from the bell tower,
and the inevitable rhythm of footsteps
that occurs when two people walk together
as friends often do

They don't see the stream of pink clouds
slip away with the rising sun,
the flag at half-staff to
memorialize a fallen hero,
or the well-marked crosswalks
meant to keep them safe

I sit on the bench
and wonder about strangers
lamenting their loneliness
while looking a screens
and I try to reason why they
are all alone in this world
socially disconnected from
others just like them

Memories in a Melody

Bubble bath in Grandma's
spotless bathtub
fresh, wind-dried nightgown
stiff like the sheets
Lawrence Welk and the
lovely Lennon sisters
heard from the front room

Goodnight, sleep tight
and pleasant dreams to you

Collecting kisses and hugs
hoping Grandpa needs
little hands to hold the
rabbit-ears for a crisp
picture and the Saturday night
fight with Howard Cosell calling
the match and yet off to bed

Here's a wish and a prayer
that every dream comes true

Tender memories of
Grandma and Grandpa
stiff starched cotton pillowcases

and Old Spice aftershave
icy cold 7-Up in tin cups
forever ago and yet in one melody
you are here in my heart

And now 'til we meet again
Adios, au revoir, auf wiedersehen.

Dogs Are Family

Looking here and
looking there
It seems that dogs
are everywhere

Coonhounds, bloodhounds,
dachshunds … a few
Foxhounds, wolfhounds,
greyhounds too.

Collies and corgis
and bassets and beagles
pointers and pit bulls
and herders and heelers

Bring on the poodles
and fine labradoodles
boxers and bulldogs
and sweet cockapoodles

No matter the owner,
the blend or the breed
Our pups are our family
as all have agreed

I Come to the Mountains

I come to the mountains
to leave the world behind
and discover my deep roots
in the beauty of the natural world

May I always find my tenacity
in the flowers and bees that
return after long bitter winters

May I always find my peace
and draw strength from
the rocks, trees, and mountains

May I always find my joy
sharing love and companionship
with others and with myself

I come to the mountains
to feed my heart and soul
and put down deep roots
to be enriched by the natural world

Eyes of Love

An old man once gave me some good advice
Don't see the world through headlines
Look through the eyes of love

It is easy to be suffocated
By deep sorrow and sadness
Instead let love prevail

Therefore, I choose to write my own headlines
"Love notes found in lunchboxes"
"Neighbors rescue a cat"

"Child brings daisies to his first-grade teacher"
"Popsicles taste better shared"
"Husband loves wife today"

Your perspective and attitude will change
If you get beyond headlines
And see with eyes of love

Step Gently Into the Night

This walk through life
is marked with steps
tentative and faltering
sometimes resulting
in spills and falls
at the dawn of a new day

As a tiny one, you learned
to walk by holding on
wobbly and wiggling
reaching out for help
as one step leads to another
guided by a radiant sun

How proud you were as
your baby steps propelled you
forward toward challenges
and new opportunities
planting steps firmly
with the sun overhead

You were blessed to have
hands to hold along the way
family, friends, strangers
needing and wanting to

keep up with the pace
through rain and shine

But as with all good things
time slowed you down and
you focused, perhaps,
less on your destination
and more on the vibrant
colors of the sunset

In time stumbling steps returned
you to that infant dependency
tentative, faltering and
reaching for the hands and
hearts of us who released you
gently into the night
                    ~ I love you, Dad

Epitaph for Produce ~ Rest In Peace

I bought you once with good intent
Veggies and fruit with money well-spent
Better eating – my thought
'Tis the reason I bought
Now I'm tossing you into the trash.

Longevity was never your finest suit
Perhaps I'm nasty with my rebuke
But couldn't you last a little bit longer
to help me be a little bit stronger?
Now I'm tossing you into the trash.

I wish I could say that I'm sorry
I'll do better next time, don't worry
Healthy eating I'll plan
I believe that I can
Now I'm tossing you into the trash.

In the Name of All That's Holy!

Do ya' remember those phrases
That momma and daddy said
When there was nothing else to say?

Phrases of futility and exasperation
Momma shakin' her head in disbelief
Maybe paired with "Lord a'mighty!"

Old phrases saved deep in memories
Daddy's gravely voice shoutin' at me
Restrained hand on his belt buckle.

"In the name of all that's holy!"
"What were ya' thinkin', child?
I swear I learnt ya' better!"

What I'd give to hear those
Voices one more time, and show
Momma and Daddy I'm doin' just fine

Walking Between the Raindrops ~ Remembering Elsa

There's an eerie silence
that follows a hurricane
Unlike the cacophony
Of songbirds singing
And screech owls bidding
Good day to the dawn
There's an eerie silence

Only dripping and tapping
And water everywhere
Dripping and splashing
from thrashed trees
and tapping of puppy toes
on sidewalks and streets
Only dripping and tapping

Walking between the raindrops
I relieve the anxiety that hides
Deep in my inner core
Accepting that Elsa is early
Foreshadowing a riotous
Hurricane season to come

Walking between the raindrops

Today I embrace the silence
Drip and splash with puppies
And simply and gratefully
Walk between the raindrops

Here Comes the Sun

The day starts at the crack of dawn
Pastel lights streak across the lawn
New sunrise

Leaves on the trees and blossoms too
Sparkle with light and morning dew
Bright sunbeams

Plate-sized blossoms facing the east
Meant to deliver birds their feast
Sunflowers

Though rain and clouds may change the sky
The sun always catches my eye
Crisp sunshine

A fresh and beautiful new day
Silent thanks and gratitude I pray
Love sunlight

Speaking to the Trees

Standing under the canopy
of lovely trees, I'm awed by
beauty that envelops
and surrounds me

Whispering leaves with secrets
catching glimpses of nests
and hiding places for
woodland creatures

Watching with envy as squirrels
leap from branch to bough
unhindered and carefree
embracing unfettered freedom

Hearing chirrups and cheeps
a sanctuary for birds
thanking heaven for trees
bearing witness of life and love

Breathing deeply, keenly aware
of each breath cleansed, restored
seedling, sapling, stately, snag
gentle giving giants

Praising heaven's grand design
revealing the hand of God
in tiny nuts and seeds, with hope
dawning each new day.

Remembering Momma

Creamed peas and tuna on warm toast
A simple meal returning to childhood
Momma said it was a Depression meal
No matter because it just made me happy

Toast smothered in creamed peas and tuna
Childhood flashing back as if it were yesterday
Meals of simple means during hard times
Happy to have something to eat.

Was it the toast or the roux in my déjà vu?
Perhaps memories of childhood or momma
It was just another meal for our family
And yet being happy means we ate today

Creamed peas and tuna on warm toast
I don't know if this is momma's or my childhood
Content to remember both the memory and the
meal
Because momma always had a way to make me
happy.

A Vision

Between the light and shadow you came,
ethereal, much like a ghost.
I know you...those eyes, that nose.
Are you a dream? A wish?
Those are my giggles.
That child is me.
A vision
of my
self.
Do I
see clearly
a woman grown?
This is my laughter,
still with dreams and wishes.
I am me... these eyes, this nose.
Not as a ghost, but flesh and blood.
From shadows I walk into the light.

Priorities

If I believe in eternity
and this life is just a flash
wouldn't I want it to be spent
with the people who matter most?

If eternity does not exist
and nothing matters past this life
shouldn't I reprioritize and be
with the people who matter most?

Eternity, regardless of my belief
is lived one moment at a time
and I wonder if am focused
on the people who matter most?

Eternity is beyond my understanding
fretting and worrying serve no purpose
instead, I will abandon that futility and
be with the people who matter most.

In the Rearview Mirror

While a glance now and then
in the rearview mirror
gives me perspective on
what is behind me,
I choose to focus instead
on what is ahead of me.
Isn't that true of life as well?

I think I am better served
by focusing on what is ahead
rather than dwelling on what's
in the rearview mirror.
I can't change what is behind me
But I can appreciate what is
Ahead of me – so why look back?

The Power of Words

I was just a tiny bit of a thing
Mesmerized by the stories
my momma and daddy would
read over and over to me

"It was night, it was dark..."
The captivating start to
my childhood favorite in
a book still on my shelf

I wonder when did these
black words on white pages
become pictures in my mind
full of color and imagery

I recall crying while reading a story
never understanding how words
so simple for a child to read and say
could elicit such strong emotion

To this day I cherish those tender
and delightfully quiet moments
spent tucked in by the window
reading and reading and reading

The Myth of Poetry

Some say that poetry
serves no purpose
that the messy jumble
of words and rhymes
come from odd people
disconnected from reality

Therein lies the myth
poetry can succinctly express
our fiercely hidden emotions
and calm our unsettled fears
It can sweetly connect us
in a community of love

Poetry in any form
can magnify our dreams
open our vast imaginations
redefine our boundaries
and let us see infinite beauty
in a multidimensional world

Together and determined
we can dispel this cruel myth
that poetry serves no purpose
Let us write and smile often
share our voices in verse
with our love of poetry